COOL CATS

British Shorthairs

by Christina Leighton

BLASTOFF!
2
READERS

BELLWETHER MEDIA • MINNEAPOLIS, MN

Note to Librarians, Teachers, and Parents:

Blastoff! Readers are carefully developed by literacy experts and combine standards-based content with developmentally appropriate text.

Level 1 provides the most support through repetition of high-frequency words, light text, predictable sentence patterns, and strong visual support.

Level 2 offers early readers a bit more challenge through varied simple sentences, increased text load, and less repetition of high-frequency words.

Level 3 advances early-fluent readers toward fluency through increased text and concept load, less reliance on visuals, longer sentences, and more literary language.

Level 4 builds reading stamina by providing more text per page, increased use of punctuation, greater variation in sentence patterns, and increasingly challenging vocabulary.

Level 5 encourages children to move from "learning to read" to "reading to learn" by providing even more text, varied writing styles, and less familiar topics.

Whichever book is right for your reader, Blastoff! Readers are the perfect books to build confidence and encourage a love of reading that will last a lifetime!

This edition first published in 2017 by Bellwether Media, Inc.

No part of this publication may be reproduced in whole or in part without written permission of the publisher. For information regarding permission, write to Bellwether Media, Inc., Attention: Permissions Department, 5357 Penn Avenue South, Minneapolis, MN 55419.

Library of Congress Cataloging-in-Publication Data

Names: Leighton, Christina, author.
Title: British Shorthairs / by Christina Leighton.
Other titles: Blastoff! Readers. 2, Cool Cats.
Description: Minneapolis, MN : Bellwether Media, Inc., [2017] | Series: Blastoff! Readers. Cool Cats | Audience: Ages 5-8. | Audience: K to grade 3. Includes bibliographical references and index.
Identifiers: LCCN 2015048424 | ISBN 9781626173958 (hardcover : alk. paper)
Subjects: LCSH: British shorthair cat-Juvenile literature. | Cat breeds-Juvenile literature.
Classification: LCC SF449.B74 L45 2017 | DDC 636.8/22-dc23
LC record available at http://lccn.loc.gov/2015048424

Printed in the United States of America, North Mankato, MN.

Table of Contents

British shorthairs are calm cats. They have wide grins.

The Cheshire Cat from *Alice's Adventures in Wonderland* may be a British shorthair!

These short-haired cats have soft **coats**. Their rounded tails are **plush**.

Sturdy bodies make British shorthairs excellent **mousers**.

History of British Shorthairs

British shorthairs are one of Great Britain's oldest cat **breeds**. They lived as street cats for hundreds of years.

Great Britain

N
W E
S

Eventually, they became indoor pets. In 1871, a British shorthair won Best in Show at the first-ever cat show!

After the world wars, British shorthairs almost disappeared. People **bred** them with other cats to save the breed.

Today, British shorthairs are found worldwide.

Shades of Blue

Many British shorthairs have **solid** blue coats. This blue is a shade of gray or silver. People call these cats British blues.

But their fur comes in other colors, too. They can be red, black, or white.

The cats can also have patterned coats.

British Shorthair Coats

solid

bi-color

calico

tabby

Some are **bi-color** or **calico**.
Others are **tabby**.

British shorthairs usually have orange, blue, or green eyes.

British Shorthair Profile

—— chubby cheeks

—— sturdy body

short,
rounded tail

Weight: 7 to 17 pounds (3 to 8 kilograms)

Life Span: 12 to 17 years

Their round cheeks are chubby.

These gentle cats want to spend time with family.

They can get too hot on laps. But they enjoy cuddling next to their owners.

British shorthairs **lounge** often.
They stretch and roll over.

After long naps, they like to play. They chase after toys!

Glossary

bi-color—a pattern that has two fur colors, one being white

bred—purposely mated two cats to make kittens with certain qualities

breeds—types of cats

calico—a pattern that has patches of white, black, and reddish brown fur

coats—the hair or fur covering some animals

lounge—to sit or rest in a lazy manner

mousers—cats that catch mice

plush—very thick and soft

solid—one color

sturdy—strongly built

tabby—a pattern that has stripes, patches, or swirls of colors

To Learn More

AT THE LIBRARY

Leaf, Christina. *American Shorthairs.* Minneapolis, Minn.: Bellwether Media, 2016.

Sexton, Colleen. *The Life Cycle of a Cat.* Minneapolis, Minn.: Bellwether Media, 2011.

Wheeler, Jill C. *British Shorthair Cats.* Minneapolis, Minn.: ABDO Pub. Co., 2012.

ON THE WEB

Learning more about British shorthairs is as easy as 1, 2, 3.

1. Go to www.factsurfer.com.

2. Enter "British shorthairs" into the search box.

3. Click the "Surf" button and you will see a list of related web sites.

With factsurfer.com, finding more information is just a click away.

Index